40 Nigerian Recipes for Home

By: Kelly Johnson

Table of Contents

- Jollof Rice
- Egusi Soup
- Pounded Yam with Egusi Soup
- Fried Plantains
- Nigerian Fried Rice
- Pepper Soup
- Moi Moi (Steamed Bean Pudding)
- Nigerian Suya (Spicy Grilled Skewered Meat)
- Akara (Bean Fritters)
- Nigerian Meat Pie
- Boli (Grilled Plantains)
- Nigerian Buns
- Ogbono Soup
- Nigerian Chin Chin
- Nigerian Chicken Stew
- Nigerian Fish Stew
- Nigerian Coconut Rice
- Nigerian Pepper Sauce
- Nigerian Okra Soup
- Nigerian Jollof Spaghetti
- Nigerian Beef Stew
- Nigerian Puff Puff
- Nigerian Akamu (Ogi/Pap)
- Nigerian Efo Riro (Vegetable Soup)
- Nigerian Fried Beans
- Nigerian Coconut Candy (Coconut Candy)
- Nigerian Moi Moi Roll
- Nigerian Banga Soup
- Nigerian Vegetable Sauce
- Nigerian Ofada Rice and Ayamase Stew
- Nigerian Afang Soup
- Nigerian Gizzdodo (Gizzard and Plantain)
- Nigerian Yam Porridge
- Nigerian Asun (Spicy Goat Meat)
- Nigerian Fisherman Soup

- Nigerian Beans Porridge (Beans Pottage)
- Nigerian Fish Roll
- Nigerian Chicken Pepper Soup
- Nigerian Prawn Stir Fry
- Nigerian Chicken Shawarma

Jollof Rice

Ingredients:

- 2 cups long-grain parboiled rice
- 1 onion, chopped
- 2-3 tomatoes, blended into a puree
- 1 red bell pepper, blended into a puree
- 1-2 Scotch bonnet peppers (adjust to taste), blended into a puree
- 3 cloves of garlic, minced
- 1 thumb-sized piece of ginger, grated
- 1 teaspoon dried thyme
- 1 teaspoon curry powder
- 1 teaspoon paprika
- 1 teaspoon dried or fresh parsley (optional)
- 2-3 tablespoons tomato paste
- 2 cups chicken or vegetable broth
- 2 tablespoons vegetable oil or palm oil
- Salt and pepper to taste
- Optional: cooked chicken, beef, or shrimp for added protein
- Optional: mixed vegetables like carrots, peas, and green beans

Instructions:

Rinse the rice in cold water until the water runs clear. Drain and set aside.

Heat the oil in a large pot over medium heat. Add the chopped onions and sauté until translucent.

Add the minced garlic and grated ginger to the pot, and cook for another minute until fragrant.

Stir in the tomato paste and cook for a few minutes to allow it to caramelize slightly.

Add the blended tomato, red bell pepper, and Scotch bonnet pepper puree to the pot. Stir well and cook for about 10-15 minutes, stirring occasionally, until the mixture reduces and thickens.

Season the mixture with thyme, curry powder, paprika, parsley (if using), salt, and pepper. Adjust seasoning to taste.

Pour in the chicken or vegetable broth and bring the mixture to a simmer.

Add the rinsed rice to the pot and stir well to combine with the tomato mixture. If using additional protein or vegetables, add them to the pot at this point.

Cover the pot with a lid and reduce the heat to low. Allow the rice to cook undisturbed for about 20-25 minutes, or until the rice is cooked through and tender, and the liquid is absorbed.

Once the rice is cooked, fluff it with a fork and serve hot.

Enjoy your delicious homemade Jollof rice! Feel free to adjust the recipe according to your preferences and dietary restrictions.

Egusi Soup

Ingredients:

- 1 cup ground egusi (melon) seeds
- 2-3 cups assorted meat/fish (such as beef, chicken, stockfish, dried fish, or shrimp)
- 1 medium onion, chopped
- 2-3 cups chopped vegetables (spinach, kale, bitter leaf, or pumpkin leaves)
- 2-3 tablespoons palm oil or vegetable oil
- 2-3 tablespoons ground crayfish
- 2-3 tablespoons ground pepper (scotch bonnet or habanero)
- 2-3 cups meat or fish stock
- Salt and seasoning cubes/powder to taste

Instructions:

If using dried fish or stockfish, soak them in hot water for about 30 minutes to soften. Drain and set aside.

Heat the palm oil or vegetable oil in a large pot over medium heat.

Add the chopped onions to the pot and sauté until translucent.

Stir in the ground egusi seeds and continue cooking, stirring frequently, until the egusi begins to release its oils and becomes slightly golden brown. This should take about 5-7 minutes.

Add the ground crayfish and ground pepper to the pot, and stir well to combine.

Pour in the meat or fish stock, and bring the mixture to a simmer.

Add the assorted meats/fish to the pot. If using tougher meats like beef, you may need to cook them for a while before adding more delicate ingredients.

Allow the soup to simmer gently for about 20-30 minutes, or until the meats/fish are cooked through and tender.

Stir in the chopped vegetables and cook for an additional 5-7 minutes, or until the vegetables are wilted and tender.

Season the soup with salt and seasoning cubes/powder to taste. Adjust seasoning as needed.

Once everything is well combined and the soup has reached your desired consistency, remove it from the heat.

Serve the Egusi soup hot, accompanied by a side of rice, fufu, or any other preferred staple.

Enjoy your flavorful and nutritious Egusi soup! Feel free to customize the recipe by adding your favorite ingredients or adjusting the seasoning to suit your taste.

Pounded Yam with Egusi Soup

Pounded Yam:

Ingredients:

- Yam (quantity depends on the number of servings, typically about 1 medium-sized yam per person)

Instructions:

Peel the yam and cut it into chunks.
Place the yam chunks in a pot of boiling water and cook until they are soft and tender.
Drain the cooked yam and transfer it to a mortar and pestle or a yam pounder.
Pound the yam until it becomes smooth and stretchy. You may need to add a little bit of water during the pounding process to achieve the desired consistency.
Once the pounded yam is smooth, shape it into balls or serve it in mounds.

Egusi Soup (using the recipe provided earlier):

Follow the instructions for making Egusi Soup as described earlier. Once the soup is ready, you can serve it alongside the pounded yam.

Serving:

To serve, place a portion of pounded yam on a plate or in a bowl, and ladle some Egusi Soup over it. The pounded yam serves as a soft and starchy base for the flavorful soup, creating a delicious and satisfying meal.

Enjoy your Pounded Yam with Egusi Soup, a traditional Nigerian delicacy!

Fried Plantains

Ingredients:

- Ripe plantains (the peel should be mostly yellow with some black spots)
- Vegetable oil or palm oil for frying
- Salt (optional)

Instructions:

Peel the plantains by cutting off both ends and slicing through the skin lengthwise. Peel away the skin and discard.
Cut the peeled plantains into slices. You can cut them into rounds or diagonal slices, depending on your preference.
Heat the vegetable oil or palm oil in a frying pan or skillet over medium-high heat.
Once the oil is hot, carefully add the plantain slices to the pan in a single layer, making sure not to overcrowd the pan.
Fry the plantains for about 2-3 minutes on each side, or until they are golden brown and caramelized.
Use a slotted spoon or spatula to transfer the fried plantains to a plate lined with paper towels to drain excess oil.
Sprinkle the fried plantains with a pinch of salt if desired while they are still hot.
Serve the fried plantains warm as a side dish or snack. They pair well with rice, beans, grilled meats, or can be enjoyed on their own.

Enjoy your crispy and sweet fried plantains! Adjust the frying time as needed to achieve your desired level of crispiness.

Nigerian Fried Rice

Ingredients:

- 3 cups cooked long-grain rice (preferably chilled or day-old rice)
- 1 cup mixed vegetables (carrots, green beans, peas, sweet corn)
- 1 onion, finely chopped
- 2-3 cloves of garlic, minced
- 1 thumb-sized piece of ginger, grated
- 1-2 scotch bonnet peppers, finely chopped (adjust to taste)
- 2 cups cooked protein (chicken, shrimp, beef, or a combination)
- 3 tablespoons vegetable oil or palm oil
- 2 tablespoons soy sauce
- 1 tablespoon curry powder
- 1 teaspoon thyme
- Salt and pepper to taste
- Optional: chopped green onions or cilantro for garnish

Instructions:

Heat the vegetable oil or palm oil in a large skillet or wok over medium heat. Add the chopped onions, minced garlic, grated ginger, and chopped scotch bonnet peppers to the skillet. Sauté until the onions are translucent and fragrant.
Stir in the mixed vegetables and cook for a few minutes until they begin to soften.
Add the cooked protein (chicken, shrimp, beef) to the skillet and stir to combine with the vegetables.
Sprinkle the curry powder, thyme, salt, and pepper over the mixture and stir well to evenly distribute the spices.
Add the cooked rice to the skillet and drizzle with soy sauce. Gently stir everything together until the rice is well-coated with the seasoning and heated through.
Cook the fried rice for an additional 5-7 minutes, stirring occasionally, to allow the flavors to meld and the rice to develop a slightly crispy texture.
Taste and adjust seasoning if needed, adding more salt, pepper, or soy sauce as desired.
Once the fried rice is cooked to your liking, remove it from the heat and transfer to a serving dish.

Garnish the Nigerian fried rice with chopped green onions or cilantro, if desired, before serving.

Enjoy your flavorful and aromatic Nigerian fried rice as a main dish or as a side to accompany your favorite Nigerian dishes!

Pepper Soup

Ingredients:

- 1 whole chicken, cut into pieces (you can also use chicken parts like thighs or drumsticks)
- 1 onion, chopped
- 2-3 cloves of garlic, minced
- 1 thumb-sized piece of ginger, grated
- 2-3 scotch bonnet peppers (adjust to taste), chopped
- 2-3 tablespoons ground crayfish (optional)
- 1 tablespoon ground dried uziza seeds (optional, for extra flavor)
- 1 teaspoon ground ehuru seeds (also known as calabash nutmeg, optional)
- 2-3 tablespoons vegetable oil or palm oil
- 6 cups water or chicken broth
- Salt and pepper to taste
- Fresh herbs such as basil or scent leaves for garnish (optional)

Instructions:

In a large pot or Dutch oven, heat the vegetable oil or palm oil over medium heat. Add the chopped onions, minced garlic, grated ginger, and chopped scotch bonnet peppers to the pot. Sauté until the onions are translucent and fragrant. Add the chicken pieces to the pot and brown them on all sides, stirring occasionally.
Once the chicken is browned, add the ground crayfish, ground dried uziza seeds (if using), and ground ehuru seeds (if using) to the pot. Stir well to coat the chicken with the spices.
Pour in the water or chicken broth, and bring the soup to a simmer.
Cover the pot and let the soup simmer for about 30-40 minutes, or until the chicken is cooked through and tender.
Taste the soup and adjust the seasoning with salt and pepper as needed.
If desired, garnish the pepper soup with fresh herbs such as basil or scent leaves before serving.
Serve the pepper soup hot as a comforting and spicy dish, either on its own or with a side of boiled white rice or yam.

Enjoy your flavorful and aromatic pepper soup! Feel free to customize the recipe by adding other ingredients like vegetables or different types of meat or seafood. Adjust the spiciness level according to your taste preferences.

Moi Moi (Steamed Bean Pudding)

Ingredients:

- 2 cups black-eyed peas (or brown beans)
- 1 medium onion, chopped
- 2-3 cloves of garlic
- 1 red bell pepper, chopped
- 1 scotch bonnet pepper (adjust to taste)
- 1/2 cup vegetable oil
- 1 teaspoon ground crayfish (optional)
- 1 teaspoon ground dried crayfish (optional)
- 1 teaspoon ground dried shrimp (optional)
- 1 teaspoon ground dried pepper (cayenne pepper)
- 1 teaspoon paprika (optional)
- 1 teaspoon ground nutmeg (optional)
- 1 teaspoon bouillon powder or cube
- Salt to taste
- 1-2 cups of water or chicken broth

Optional Additions:

- Hard-boiled eggs, peeled and sliced
- Cooked fish or shredded chicken
- Vegetables such as chopped spinach or kale

Instructions:

Rinse the black-eyed peas or brown beans thoroughly and soak them in water for at least 4 hours or overnight to soften.
Drain the soaked beans and transfer them to a blender or food processor.
Add the chopped onion, garlic cloves, red bell pepper, scotch bonnet pepper, and vegetable oil to the blender.
Blend the mixture until smooth, adding water as needed to achieve a smooth consistency. The batter should be thick but pourable.
Transfer the blended mixture to a large mixing bowl.
Add the ground crayfish, ground dried shrimp, ground dried pepper, paprika, ground nutmeg, bouillon powder or cube, and salt to taste. Stir well to combine.

If using any optional additions such as hard-boiled eggs, cooked fish, or vegetables, fold them into the batter.

Grease small containers or ramekins with oil or line them with banana leaves.

Pour the batter into the greased containers, filling them about two-thirds full.

Prepare a steamer by adding water to the bottom pot and bringing it to a boil.

Arrange the filled containers in the steamer and cover with a lid.

Steam the Moi Moi over medium heat for about 45 minutes to 1 hour, or until set and cooked through. Insert a toothpick or knife into the center of the Moi Moi; if it comes out clean, it's done.

Once cooked, remove the Moi Moi from the steamer and let them cool slightly before unmolding.

Serve the Moi Moi warm or at room temperature, garnished with additional sliced vegetables or hard-boiled eggs if desired.

Enjoy your homemade Moi Moi as a delicious and nutritious snack or side dish! Adjust the seasoning and spice level according to your taste preferences.

Nigerian Suya (Spicy Grilled Skewered Meat)

Ingredients:

- 1 lb beef sirloin, chicken breast, or liver, thinly sliced
- Skewers (wooden or metal)
- 1/4 cup groundnut (peanut) powder
- 1 tablespoon ground ginger
- 1 tablespoon ground paprika
- 1 tablespoon ground cayenne pepper (adjust to taste)
- 1 tablespoon onion powder
- 1 tablespoon garlic powder
- 1 tablespoon bouillon powder or cube, crumbled
- Salt to taste
- Vegetable oil for brushing

For Serving:

- Sliced onions
- Sliced tomatoes
- Sliced cucumber
- Spicy pepper sauce (such as Nigerian pepper sauce or Suya spice mix)

Instructions:

If using wooden skewers, soak them in water for at least 30 minutes to prevent burning during grilling.
In a bowl, combine the groundnut powder, ground ginger, ground paprika, ground cayenne pepper, onion powder, garlic powder, bouillon powder or cube, and salt to taste. This mixture is known as the Suya spice rub.
Thread the thinly sliced meat onto the skewers, making sure to leave a little space between each piece for even cooking.
Brush the meat skewers with vegetable oil to help the spice rub adhere.
Generously sprinkle the Suya spice rub over the meat skewers, coating them on all sides. Press the spice rub into the meat to ensure it sticks.
Preheat a grill or grill pan over medium-high heat.
Once the grill is hot, place the meat skewers on the grill and cook for about 3-4 minutes on each side, or until the meat is cooked through and has grill marks.

Remove the cooked Suya skewers from the grill and let them rest for a few minutes.

Serve the Suya skewers hot, accompanied by sliced onions, tomatoes, cucumber, and spicy pepper sauce on the side.

Enjoy your delicious and spicy Nigerian Suya as a snack or appetizer! Adjust the spice level according to your taste preferences, and feel free to experiment with different types of meat or cuts.

Akara (Bean Fritters)

Ingredients:

- 2 cups black-eyed peas or brown beans
- 1 small onion, chopped
- 1-2 scotch bonnet peppers (adjust to taste), chopped
- Salt to taste
- Vegetable oil for frying

Instructions:

Rinse the black-eyed peas or brown beans thoroughly and soak them in water for at least 4 hours or overnight to soften.

After soaking, drain the beans and transfer them to a blender or food processor. Blend the beans until you get a smooth paste, adding a little water if needed to help with blending. The consistency should be thick but pourable.

Transfer the blended bean paste to a large mixing bowl.

Add the chopped onion, chopped scotch bonnet peppers, and salt to the bean paste. Stir well to combine.

Heat vegetable oil in a deep frying pan or pot over medium-high heat.

Once the oil is hot, use a spoon to scoop up some of the bean mixture and carefully drop it into the hot oil. You can also use your hand to shape the mixture into small balls before frying.

Fry the Akara in batches, making sure not to overcrowd the pan. Fry until golden brown and crispy, turning occasionally to ensure even cooking. This should take about 3-4 minutes per batch.

Once the Akara is cooked, remove it from the oil using a slotted spoon and transfer it to a plate lined with paper towels to drain excess oil.

Repeat the frying process with the remaining bean mixture until all the Akara is cooked.

Serve the Akara hot as a snack or breakfast dish, accompanied by pap (cornmeal porridge), bread, or your preferred side.

Enjoy your homemade Akara, crispy on the outside and soft on the inside, bursting with flavor from the onions and peppers! Adjust the spiciness level according to your taste preferences by adding more or fewer scotch bonnet peppers.

Nigerian Meat Pie

Ingredients:

For the pastry:

- 3 cups all-purpose flour
- 1 cup cold butter or margarine, cubed
- 1 teaspoon baking powder
- 1/2 teaspoon salt
- 1/2 cup cold water (approximately)

For the filling:

- 1 lb ground beef or minced meat
- 1 onion, finely chopped
- 2-3 cloves garlic, minced
- 1 carrot, finely diced
- 1 medium potato, peeled and finely diced
- 1/2 cup frozen peas
- 1 tablespoon tomato paste
- 1 teaspoon curry powder
- 1/2 teaspoon thyme
- Salt and pepper to taste
- Vegetable oil for frying
- Hard-boiled eggs, sliced (optional)

Instructions:

Preheat your oven to 350°F (175°C).
In a large mixing bowl, combine the flour, baking powder, and salt. Add the cubed butter or margarine, and using your fingertips, rub the butter into the flour until the mixture resembles breadcrumbs.
Gradually add the cold water to the flour mixture, a little at a time, and knead until a smooth dough forms. Be careful not to overwork the dough.
Cover the dough with plastic wrap or a clean kitchen towel and let it rest while you prepare the filling.

In a large skillet or frying pan, heat a little vegetable oil over medium heat. Add the chopped onion and minced garlic, and sauté until translucent.

Add the ground beef or minced meat to the skillet, and cook until browned, breaking it up with a spoon as it cooks.

Stir in the diced carrot, diced potato, frozen peas, tomato paste, curry powder, thyme, salt, and pepper. Cook for a few minutes until the vegetables are tender but still slightly crisp. Remove from heat and let the filling cool slightly.

Roll out the pastry dough on a lightly floured surface to about 1/4 inch thickness. Use a round cutter or glass to cut out circles of dough for the meat pies.

Place a spoonful of the meat filling onto one half of each pastry circle, leaving a small border around the edges. If using hard-boiled eggs, place a slice on top of the filling.

Fold the other half of the pastry circle over the filling to form a semi-circle, and use a fork to crimp the edges together to seal the pies.

Transfer the assembled meat pies onto a baking sheet lined with parchment paper.

Beat an egg and brush the tops of the meat pies with the egg wash for a golden finish (optional).

Bake the meat pies in the preheated oven for 25-30 minutes, or until they are golden brown and cooked through.

Remove from the oven and let the meat pies cool slightly before serving.

Enjoy your homemade Nigerian meat pies as a tasty snack or appetizer! They can be enjoyed warm or at room temperature.

Boli (Grilled Plantains)

Ingredients:

- Ripe plantains (choose plantains that are yellow with black spots)
- Vegetable oil or melted butter (for brushing)
- Salt (optional)

Instructions:

Preheat your grill to medium-high heat. You can also use a barbecue grill or a stovetop grill pan.

While the grill is heating up, prepare the plantains. Peel the plantains and cut them into halves or quarters lengthwise, depending on your preference.

Lightly brush the plantain pieces with vegetable oil or melted butter on both sides. This will help prevent sticking and promote even grilling.

If desired, sprinkle a little salt over the plantains for added flavor. This step is optional, as the natural sweetness of the plantains is often sufficient.

Once the grill is hot, place the plantain pieces directly on the grill grates. Grill for about 3-5 minutes on each side, or until the plantains are tender and grill marks form.

Keep an eye on the plantains and flip them occasionally to ensure even cooking and to prevent burning.

Once the plantains are grilled to your liking and have softened, remove them from the grill and transfer them to a serving plate.

Serve the boli hot, either on its own or with a side of spicy pepper sauce or roasted peanuts for dipping.

Enjoy your homemade boli as a delicious and satisfying snack or side dish!

Boli is best served fresh off the grill while still warm. The grilling process enhances the natural sweetness of the plantains and adds a delightful smoky flavor. Feel free to customize your boli by adding additional seasonings or toppings according to your taste preferences.

Nigerian Buns

Ingredients:

- 2 cups all-purpose flour
- 1/2 cup sugar (adjust to taste)
- 1 teaspoon baking powder
- 1/4 teaspoon salt
- 1/4 teaspoon nutmeg (optional)
- 1/4 cup milk
- 2 large eggs
- 2 tablespoons melted butter or vegetable oil
- Vegetable oil for frying

Instructions:

In a large mixing bowl, combine the all-purpose flour, sugar, baking powder, salt, and nutmeg (if using). Mix well to combine.
In a separate bowl, whisk together the milk, eggs, and melted butter or vegetable oil until well combined.
Pour the wet ingredients into the dry ingredients and stir until a thick batter forms. The batter should be thick enough to scoop with a spoon but still drop easily.
Heat vegetable oil in a deep fryer or large pot to 350°F (180°C).
Using a spoon or ice cream scoop, scoop out portions of the batter and drop them carefully into the hot oil. You can also use your hands to shape the batter into balls before dropping them into the oil.
Fry the buns in batches, making sure not to overcrowd the pot, until they are golden brown and cooked through. This should take about 3-5 minutes per batch.
Use a slotted spoon to remove the fried buns from the oil and transfer them to a plate lined with paper towels to drain excess oil.
Allow the buns to cool slightly before serving.
Serve the Nigerian buns warm as a snack or dessert. They are best enjoyed freshly fried and can be served on their own or with a cup of tea or coffee.

Enjoy your homemade Nigerian buns, with their soft, fluffy interior and deliciously sweet flavor! Adjust the amount of sugar according to your taste preferences, and feel free to add other flavorings such as vanilla extract or grated citrus zest for variation.

Ogbono Soup

Ingredients:

- 1/2 cup ground ogbono seeds
- Assorted meats (such as beef, chicken, or goat meat), cut into bite-sized pieces
- 1/2 cup dried fish or stockfish, soaked in water until softened
- 1 onion, chopped
- 2-3 cups chopped vegetables (such as spinach, kale, or ugu leaves)
- 2-3 tablespoons palm oil or vegetable oil
- 2-3 tablespoons ground crayfish
- 1-2 scotch bonnet peppers (adjust to taste), chopped
- 1 teaspoon ground dry pepper (cayenne pepper)
- 1 teaspoon ground dried uziza seeds (optional, for extra flavor)
- 1 teaspoon ground dried ehuru seeds (also known as calabash nutmeg, optional)
- 2-3 cups meat or fish stock
- Salt and seasoning cubes/powder to taste

Instructions:

In a pot, heat the palm oil or vegetable oil over medium heat.
Add the chopped onion to the pot and sauté until translucent.
Stir in the ground ogbono seeds and cook for a few minutes, stirring constantly, until they begin to release their oils and become slightly sticky.
Add the ground crayfish, chopped scotch bonnet peppers, ground dry pepper, ground dried uziza seeds (if using), and ground dried ehuru seeds (if using) to the pot. Stir well to combine.
Pour in the meat or fish stock, and bring the mixture to a simmer.
Add the assorted meats and soaked dried fish or stockfish to the pot. If using tougher meats like beef, you may need to cook them for a while before adding more delicate ingredients.
Allow the soup to simmer gently for about 20-30 minutes, or until the meats are cooked through and tender.
Stir in the chopped vegetables and cook for an additional 5-7 minutes, or until the vegetables are wilted and tender.
Season the soup with salt and seasoning cubes/powder to taste. Adjust seasoning as needed.
Once everything is well combined and the soup has reached your desired consistency, remove it from the heat.

Serve the Ogbono soup hot, accompanied by a side of fufu, pounded yam, or your preferred staple.

Enjoy your flavorful and nutritious Ogbono soup, a comforting and satisfying dish that's perfect for any occasion! Feel free to adjust the recipe by adding your favorite ingredients or tweaking the seasoning to suit your taste preferences.

Nigerian Chin Chin

Ingredients:

- 2 cups all-purpose flour
- 1/2 cup granulated sugar
- 1/4 teaspoon baking powder
- 1/4 teaspoon salt
- 1/4 teaspoon ground nutmeg (optional)
- 1/4 cup unsalted butter, softened
- 1 large egg
- 1/4 cup milk or water
- Vegetable oil for frying

Instructions:

In a large mixing bowl, sift together the all-purpose flour, granulated sugar, baking powder, salt, and ground nutmeg (if using). Mix well to combine.
Add the softened unsalted butter to the dry ingredients. Use your fingertips to rub the butter into the flour mixture until it resembles coarse breadcrumbs.
In a separate bowl, lightly beat the egg and add it to the flour mixture. Stir until the egg is fully incorporated into the dough.
Gradually add the milk or water to the dough, a little at a time, and knead until a smooth, firm dough forms. You may not need to use all of the liquid, so add it slowly until you achieve the desired consistency.
Once the dough is formed, divide it into smaller portions and roll each portion out on a lightly floured surface to about 1/4 inch thickness.
Use a knife or cookie cutter to cut the rolled-out dough into small squares, rectangles, or any desired shapes.
Heat vegetable oil in a deep fryer or large pot to about 350°F (175°C).
Carefully drop the cut-out pieces of dough into the hot oil, making sure not to overcrowd the pot. Fry the Chin Chin in batches until they are golden brown and crispy, stirring occasionally to ensure even cooking. This should take about 3-5 minutes per batch.
Once the Chin Chin is cooked, use a slotted spoon to remove them from the oil and transfer them to a plate lined with paper towels to drain excess oil.
Allow the fried Chin Chin to cool completely before serving. They will continue to crisp up as they cool.

Serve the Nigerian Chin Chin as a delicious snack or dessert. Store any leftovers in an airtight container at room temperature for up to a week.

Enjoy your homemade Nigerian Chin Chin, with its crunchy texture and delightful sweetness! Feel free to customize the recipe by adding other flavorings such as vanilla extract or grated citrus zest for variation.

Nigerian Chicken Stew

Ingredients:

- 1 whole chicken, cut into pieces
- 2 onions, chopped
- 3-4 tomatoes, chopped
- 2-3 bell peppers (red, yellow, or green), chopped
- 2-3 scotch bonnet peppers (adjust to taste), chopped
- 3 cloves of garlic, minced
- 1 thumb-sized piece of ginger, grated
- 1/4 cup vegetable oil or palm oil
- 2 tablespoons tomato paste
- 1 teaspoon curry powder
- 1 teaspoon thyme
- 1 teaspoon paprika
- 2 cups chicken broth or water
- Salt and pepper to taste
- Fresh cilantro or parsley for garnish (optional)

Instructions:

Heat vegetable oil or palm oil in a large pot or Dutch oven over medium heat.
Add chopped onions to the pot and sauté until translucent.
Stir in minced garlic and grated ginger, and cook for another minute until fragrant.
Add chopped tomatoes, bell peppers, and scotch bonnet peppers to the pot.
Cook for about 10-15 minutes, stirring occasionally, until the vegetables soften and release their juices.
Stir in tomato paste, curry powder, thyme, and paprika. Cook for a few more minutes to allow the flavors to meld.
Add the chicken pieces to the pot and coat them with the tomato mixture.
Pour in chicken broth or water, enough to cover the chicken pieces. Bring the mixture to a simmer.
Cover the pot and let the stew cook for about 30-40 minutes, or until the chicken is cooked through and tender, and the sauce has thickened.
Taste the stew and adjust the seasoning with salt and pepper as needed.
Once the chicken stew is cooked, remove it from the heat and let it cool slightly before serving.

Garnish the Nigerian chicken stew with fresh cilantro or parsley, if desired, before serving.

Serve the Nigerian chicken stew hot with rice, yams, plantains, or any other preferred side dish. Enjoy the rich and flavorful taste of this classic Nigerian dish!

Nigerian Fish Stew

Ingredients:

- 1 lb fish fillets (such as tilapia, catfish, or mackerel), cut into chunks
- 2 onions, chopped
- 3-4 tomatoes, chopped
- 2-3 bell peppers (red, yellow, or green), chopped
- 2-3 scotch bonnet peppers (adjust to taste), chopped
- 3 cloves of garlic, minced
- 1 thumb-sized piece of ginger, grated
- 1/4 cup vegetable oil or palm oil
- 2 tablespoons tomato paste
- 1 teaspoon curry powder
- 1 teaspoon thyme
- 1 teaspoon paprika
- 2 cups fish broth or water
- Salt and pepper to taste
- Fresh cilantro or parsley for garnish (optional)

Instructions:

Heat vegetable oil or palm oil in a large pot or Dutch oven over medium heat.
Add chopped onions to the pot and sauté until translucent.
Stir in minced garlic and grated ginger, and cook for another minute until fragrant.
Add chopped tomatoes, bell peppers, and scotch bonnet peppers to the pot.
Cook for about 10-15 minutes, stirring occasionally, until the vegetables soften and release their juices.
Stir in tomato paste, curry powder, thyme, and paprika. Cook for a few more minutes to allow the flavors to meld.
Add the fish chunks to the pot and coat them with the tomato mixture.
Pour in fish broth or water, enough to cover the fish chunks. Bring the mixture to a simmer.
Cover the pot and let the stew cook for about 20-25 minutes, or until the fish is cooked through and tender, and the sauce has thickened.
Taste the stew and adjust the seasoning with salt and pepper as needed.
Once the fish stew is cooked, remove it from the heat and let it cool slightly before serving.

Garnish the Nigerian fish stew with fresh cilantro or parsley, if desired, before serving.

Serve the Nigerian fish stew hot with rice, yams, plantains, or any other preferred side dish. Enjoy the rich and flavorful taste of this classic Nigerian dish!

Nigerian Coconut Rice

Ingredients:

- 2 cups long-grain white rice
- 1 can (13.5 oz) coconut milk
- 1 cup chicken broth or water
- 1 onion, finely chopped
- 2 cloves of garlic, minced
- 1 thumb-sized piece of ginger, grated
- 1-2 scotch bonnet peppers (adjust to taste), chopped
- 1 red bell pepper, chopped
- 1 cup chopped mixed vegetables (such as carrots, peas, and green beans)
- 2 tablespoons vegetable oil or coconut oil
- 1 teaspoon curry powder
- 1 teaspoon thyme
- Salt and pepper to taste
- Fresh cilantro or parsley for garnish (optional)

Instructions:

Rinse the rice under cold water until the water runs clear. Drain and set aside.
In a large pot or Dutch oven, heat vegetable oil or coconut oil over medium heat.
Add chopped onions to the pot and sauté until translucent.
Stir in minced garlic, grated ginger, and chopped scotch bonnet peppers. Cook for another minute until fragrant.
Add chopped red bell pepper and mixed vegetables to the pot. Cook for about 5 minutes, stirring occasionally, until the vegetables are slightly softened.
Stir in curry powder and thyme, and cook for another minute to toast the spices.
Pour in the coconut milk and chicken broth (or water) into the pot. Bring the mixture to a gentle simmer.
Add the rinsed rice to the pot and stir well to combine with the coconut milk mixture.
Season with salt and pepper to taste. Cover the pot with a tight-fitting lid and reduce the heat to low.
Let the coconut rice simmer gently for about 15-20 minutes, or until the rice is cooked through and has absorbed the liquid. Avoid stirring the rice too much to prevent it from becoming mushy.

Once the rice is cooked, remove the pot from the heat and let it sit, covered, for a few minutes to steam.

Fluff the rice with a fork and garnish with fresh cilantro or parsley, if desired, before serving.

Serve the Nigerian Coconut Rice hot as a delicious and fragrant side dish. It pairs well with a variety of Nigerian mains such as grilled chicken, fish, or beef stew. Enjoy the rich and creamy taste of this classic Nigerian dish!

Nigerian Pepper Sauce

Ingredients:

- 4 large bell peppers (red, yellow, or green), chopped
- 4 ripe tomatoes, chopped
- 2 onions, chopped
- 2-3 scotch bonnet peppers (adjust to taste), chopped
- 3 cloves of garlic, minced
- 1 thumb-sized piece of ginger, grated
- 1/4 cup vegetable oil or palm oil
- 1 teaspoon paprika (optional, for color)
- 1 teaspoon curry powder (optional, for flavor)
- Salt to taste
- Fresh cilantro or parsley for garnish (optional)

Instructions:

Heat vegetable oil or palm oil in a large saucepan or skillet over medium heat.
Add chopped onions to the pot and sauté until translucent.
Stir in minced garlic and grated ginger, and cook for another minute until fragrant.
Add chopped bell peppers, tomatoes, and scotch bonnet peppers to the pot.
Cook for about 10-15 minutes, stirring occasionally, until the vegetables are softened and start to break down.
Stir in paprika and curry powder, if using, and cook for another minute to enhance the flavors.
Use an immersion blender or transfer the mixture to a blender or food processor, and blend until smooth. Be careful when blending hot liquids.
Return the blended mixture to the pot and season with salt to taste. Cook for an additional 5-10 minutes to thicken the sauce and allow the flavors to meld.
Once the Pepper Sauce reaches your desired consistency, remove it from the heat.
Garnish the Nigerian Pepper Sauce with fresh cilantro or parsley, if desired, before serving.

Serve the Nigerian Pepper Sauce hot or at room temperature as a spicy and flavorful condiment alongside your favorite Nigerian dishes. Store any leftovers in an airtight container in the refrigerator for up to a week. Enjoy the bold and fiery taste of this classic Nigerian condiment!

Nigerian Okra Soup

Ingredients:

- 2 cups chopped okra (fresh or frozen)
- Assorted meats (such as beef, chicken, or goat meat), cut into bite-sized pieces
- 1 onion, chopped
- 2-3 tomatoes, chopped
- 2-3 scotch bonnet peppers (adjust to taste), chopped
- 3 cloves of garlic, minced
- 1 thumb-sized piece of ginger, grated
- 1/4 cup palm oil or vegetable oil
- 2 cups chopped spinach or other leafy greens (such as ugu leaves)
- 2 cups meat or vegetable broth
- Salt and pepper to taste
- Ground crayfish or shrimp (optional, for extra flavor)
- Ground dried fish or smoked fish (optional)
- Seasoning cubes or powder (optional)

Instructions:

In a large pot or Dutch oven, heat palm oil or vegetable oil over medium heat.
Add chopped onions to the pot and sauté until translucent.
Stir in minced garlic and grated ginger, and cook for another minute until fragrant.
Add chopped tomatoes and scotch bonnet peppers to the pot. Cook for about 10-15 minutes, stirring occasionally, until the tomatoes break down and release their juices.
Add chopped okra to the pot and stir well to combine with the tomato mixture. Cook for a few minutes until the okra is slightly softened.
Add the assorted meats to the pot and stir to coat them with the okra and tomato mixture.
Pour in meat or vegetable broth into the pot, enough to cover the ingredients. Bring the mixture to a gentle simmer.
Cook the Okra Soup for about 20-30 minutes, or until the meats are cooked through and tender, and the soup has thickened slightly.
Stir in chopped spinach or other leafy greens to the pot and cook for an additional 5-10 minutes, or until the greens are wilted and tender.

Season the soup with salt, pepper, and any optional ingredients such as ground crayfish, ground dried fish, or seasoning cubes or powder, according to your taste preferences.

Once the Okra Soup is cooked to your liking, remove it from the heat.

Serve the Nigerian Okra Soup hot, accompanied by a side of fufu, pounded yam, or rice.

Enjoy the delicious and nutritious Nigerian Okra Soup, filled with the flavors of fresh vegetables and assorted meats! Feel free to customize the recipe by adding other ingredients or adjusting the seasoning according to your taste preferences.

Nigerian Jollof Spaghetti

Ingredients:

- 250g spaghetti noodles
- 1 onion, finely chopped
- 2-3 tomatoes, blended into a puree
- 1 red bell pepper, blended into a puree
- 1 green bell pepper, blended into a puree
- 2-3 scotch bonnet peppers (adjust to taste), blended into a puree
- 3 cloves of garlic, minced
- 1 thumb-sized piece of ginger, grated
- 1/4 cup vegetable oil or palm oil
- 1 teaspoon curry powder
- 1 teaspoon thyme
- 1 teaspoon paprika
- 2 cups chicken broth or water
- Salt and pepper to taste
- Optional: cooked chicken, beef, or shrimp for added protein
- Fresh cilantro or parsley for garnish (optional)

Instructions:

Cook the spaghetti noodles according to the package instructions until al dente. Drain and set aside.
In a large pot or Dutch oven, heat vegetable oil or palm oil over medium heat.
Add finely chopped onions to the pot and sauté until translucent.
Stir in minced garlic and grated ginger, and cook for another minute until fragrant.
Add the blended tomato puree, red bell pepper puree, green bell pepper puree, and scotch bonnet pepper puree to the pot. Cook for about 10-15 minutes, stirring occasionally, until the mixture thickens and the oil starts to separate.
Stir in curry powder, thyme, and paprika, and cook for another minute to enhance the flavors.
Pour in chicken broth or water into the pot, and bring the mixture to a gentle simmer.
Add the cooked spaghetti noodles to the pot and stir well to coat them with the Jollof sauce. If using cooked chicken, beef, or shrimp, add it to the pot at this point.

Cover the pot and let the Jollof Spaghetti simmer for about 5-10 minutes, stirring occasionally, to allow the flavors to meld together.

Taste the Jollof Spaghetti and adjust the seasoning with salt and pepper as needed.

Once the Jollof Spaghetti is heated through and the flavors are well combined, remove it from the heat.

Serve the Nigerian Jollof Spaghetti hot, garnished with fresh cilantro or parsley, if desired.

Enjoy the delicious and colorful Nigerian Jollof Spaghetti as a satisfying and comforting meal! Feel free to customize the recipe by adding other ingredients such as vegetables or protein according to your taste preferences.

Nigerian Beef Stew

Ingredients:

- 1 lb beef stew meat, cut into bite-sized pieces
- 2 onions, chopped
- 3-4 tomatoes, chopped
- 2-3 bell peppers (red, yellow, or green), chopped
- 2-3 scotch bonnet peppers (adjust to taste), chopped
- 3 cloves of garlic, minced
- 1 thumb-sized piece of ginger, grated
- 1/4 cup vegetable oil or palm oil
- 2 tablespoons tomato paste
- 1 teaspoon curry powder
- 1 teaspoon thyme
- 1 teaspoon paprika
- 2 cups beef broth or water
- Salt and pepper to taste
- Fresh cilantro or parsley for garnish (optional)

Instructions:

In a large pot or Dutch oven, heat vegetable oil or palm oil over medium heat.
Add chopped onions to the pot and sauté until translucent.
Stir in minced garlic and grated ginger, and cook for another minute until fragrant.
Add chopped tomatoes, bell peppers, and scotch bonnet peppers to the pot.
Cook for about 10-15 minutes, stirring occasionally, until the vegetables are softened and release their juices.
Stir in tomato paste, curry powder, thyme, and paprika. Cook for a few more minutes to allow the flavors to meld.
Add the beef stew meat to the pot and coat it with the tomato mixture.
Pour in beef broth or water into the pot, enough to cover the beef stew meat. Bring the mixture to a gentle simmer.
Cover the pot and let the stew cook for about 1 to 1.5 hours, or until the beef is tender and cooked through. Stir occasionally and add more broth or water if needed to prevent the stew from drying out.
Taste the stew and adjust the seasoning with salt and pepper as needed.
Once the beef stew is cooked to your liking and has reached your desired consistency, remove it from the heat.

Garnish the Nigerian Beef Stew with fresh cilantro or parsley, if desired, before serving.

Serve the Nigerian Beef Stew hot with rice, yams, plantains, or any other preferred side dish. Enjoy the rich and flavorful taste of this classic Nigerian dish!

Nigerian Puff Puff

Ingredients:

- 2 cups all-purpose flour
- 1/2 cup granulated sugar (adjust to taste)
- 1 teaspoon instant yeast
- 1 cup warm water
- 1/2 teaspoon ground nutmeg (optional)
- Vegetable oil for frying

Instructions:

In a large mixing bowl, combine the all-purpose flour, sugar, instant yeast, and ground nutmeg (if using). Mix well to combine.
Gradually add the warm water to the flour mixture, stirring continuously, until a thick batter forms. The batter should be smooth and free of lumps.
Cover the bowl with a clean kitchen towel or plastic wrap and let the batter rest in a warm place for about 1 hour, or until it doubles in size and becomes frothy.
In a deep pot or fryer, heat vegetable oil over medium heat until it reaches about 350°F (175°C).
Using a spoon or your hand, scoop up small portions of the batter and carefully drop them into the hot oil. You can also use a small ice cream scoop for uniform sizes.
Fry the puff puff in batches, making sure not to overcrowd the pot. Cook until they are golden brown and puffed up, turning them occasionally to ensure even cooking. This should take about 2-3 minutes per batch.
Use a slotted spoon to remove the fried puff puff from the oil and transfer them to a plate lined with paper towels to drain excess oil.
Repeat the frying process with the remaining batter until all the puff puff are cooked.
Allow the puff puff to cool slightly before serving.
Serve the Nigerian puff puff warm as a delicious snack or dessert. They are best enjoyed fresh and can be served on their own or dusted with powdered sugar or cinnamon sugar for extra sweetness.

Enjoy your homemade Nigerian puff puff, with their soft and airy texture and delightful sweetness! Feel free to customize the recipe by adding other flavorings such as vanilla extract or grated citrus zest for variation.

Nigerian Akamu (Ogi/Pap)

Ingredients:

- 1 cup cornmeal (also known as corn flour or maize flour)
- 4 cups water
- Sugar or honey to taste (optional)
- Milk (optional)
- Flavorings such as vanilla extract or cinnamon (optional)

Instructions:

In a bowl, mix the cornmeal with a small amount of water to form a smooth paste. Ensure there are no lumps.
In a large pot, bring the remaining water to a boil over medium-high heat.
Slowly pour the cornmeal paste into the boiling water, stirring constantly to prevent lumps from forming.
Reduce the heat to low and continue stirring the mixture. Cook for about 10-15 minutes, or until the mixture thickens to a smooth consistency, similar to a thin pudding.
Cover the pot and let the mixture simmer for an additional 5-10 minutes, stirring occasionally to prevent burning. This helps to cook the cornmeal thoroughly and develop its flavor.
Once the Akamu has reached the desired consistency, remove it from the heat and let it cool slightly.
If desired, sweeten the Akamu with sugar or honey to taste. You can also add milk for a creamier texture and flavor, and flavorings such as vanilla extract or cinnamon for extra taste.
Serve the Nigerian Akamu warm or chilled in bowls or cups. It can be enjoyed on its own as a breakfast dish or paired with Nigerian snacks such as Akara (bean fritters) or Moi Moi (steamed bean pudding).
Leftover Akamu can be stored in the refrigerator for up to a few days. Simply reheat it before serving.

Enjoy the smooth and creamy texture of Nigerian Akamu, a comforting and nutritious breakfast option that's perfect for starting your day! Adjust the sweetness and flavorings according to your taste preferences.

Nigerian Efo Riro (Vegetable Soup)

Ingredients:

- Assorted meats or seafood (such as beef, chicken, shrimp, or fish), cut into bite-sized pieces
- 2-3 cups chopped spinach or other leafy greens (such as kale or ugu leaves)
- 1 onion, chopped
- 2-3 tomatoes, chopped
- 2-3 bell peppers (red, yellow, or green), chopped
- 2-3 scotch bonnet peppers (adjust to taste), chopped
- 3 cloves of garlic, minced
- 1 thumb-sized piece of ginger, grated
- 1/4 cup palm oil or vegetable oil
- 2 tablespoons tomato paste
- 1 teaspoon ground crayfish or shrimp (optional, for extra flavor)
- 1 teaspoon ground dried fish or smoked fish (optional)
- 2 cups chicken broth or water
- Salt and pepper to taste
- Ground cayenne pepper or chili flakes (optional, for extra heat)
- Fresh cilantro or parsley for garnish (optional)

Instructions:

In a large pot or Dutch oven, heat palm oil or vegetable oil over medium heat.
Add chopped onions to the pot and sauté until translucent.
Stir in minced garlic and grated ginger, and cook for another minute until fragrant.
Add chopped tomatoes, bell peppers, and scotch bonnet peppers to the pot.
Cook for about 10-15 minutes, stirring occasionally, until the vegetables soften and release their juices.
Stir in tomato paste and ground crayfish or shrimp, if using. Cook for a few more minutes to allow the flavors to meld.
Add the assorted meats or seafood to the pot and coat them with the tomato mixture.
Pour in chicken broth or water into the pot, enough to cover the ingredients. Bring the mixture to a gentle simmer.
Cover the pot and let the soup cook for about 20-30 minutes, or until the meats or seafood are cooked through and tender.

Stir in chopped spinach or other leafy greens to the pot and cook for an additional 5-10 minutes, or until the greens are wilted and tender.
Season the soup with salt, pepper, and ground cayenne pepper or chili flakes, if using, to taste.
Once the Efo Riro is cooked to your liking, remove it from the heat.
Serve the Nigerian Efo Riro hot with rice, pounded yam, or any other preferred side dish.

Enjoy the delicious and nutritious Nigerian Efo Riro, filled with the flavors of assorted meats or seafood and fresh vegetables! Feel free to customize the recipe by adding other ingredients or adjusting the seasoning according to your taste preferences.

Nigerian Fried Beans

Ingredients:

- 2 cups black-eyed peas (also known as brown beans), soaked overnight or for at least 4 hours
- 1 onion, chopped
- 2-3 tomatoes, chopped
- 2-3 scotch bonnet peppers (adjust to taste), chopped
- 3 cloves of garlic, minced
- 1 thumb-sized piece of ginger, grated
- 1/4 cup palm oil or vegetable oil
- 1 teaspoon ground crayfish (optional, for extra flavor)
- 1 teaspoon ground dried fish or smoked fish (optional)
- Salt and pepper to taste
- Fresh cilantro or parsley for garnish (optional)

Instructions:

Drain and rinse the soaked black-eyed peas thoroughly. Place them in a large pot and cover with water. Bring to a boil over medium-high heat and cook until tender, about 30-40 minutes. Drain and set aside.

In a large skillet or frying pan, heat palm oil or vegetable oil over medium heat.

Add chopped onions to the skillet and sauté until translucent.

Stir in minced garlic and grated ginger, and cook for another minute until fragrant.

Add chopped tomatoes and scotch bonnet peppers to the skillet. Cook for about 10-15 minutes, stirring occasionally, until the tomatoes break down and release their juices.

Stir in ground crayfish and ground dried fish or smoked fish, if using. Cook for a few more minutes to allow the flavors to meld.

Add the cooked black-eyed peas to the skillet and stir well to combine with the tomato mixture. Use a potato masher or fork to mash some of the beans slightly, leaving some whole for texture.

Season the fried beans with salt and pepper to taste. Continue cooking for another 5-10 minutes, stirring occasionally, until the flavors are well combined.

Once the fried beans reach your desired consistency and flavor, remove them from the heat.

Garnish the Nigerian Fried Beans with fresh cilantro or parsley, if desired, before serving.

Serve the Nigerian Fried Beans hot as a delicious and satisfying meal or side dish. Enjoy the rich and flavorful taste of this classic Nigerian dish! Feel free to customize the recipe by adding other ingredients such as bell peppers, spinach, or crayfish according to your taste preferences.

Nigerian Coconut Candy (Coconut Candy)

Ingredients:

- 2 cups grated coconut (fresh or desiccated)
- 1 cup granulated sugar
- 1/2 cup water
- 1/4 teaspoon vanilla extract (optional)
- Pinch of salt

Instructions:

In a large skillet or frying pan, combine the sugar and water. Heat the mixture over medium heat, stirring constantly, until the sugar is completely dissolved. Add the grated coconut to the sugar syrup in the skillet. Stir well to combine. Continue cooking the mixture over medium heat, stirring frequently, until it starts to thicken and turn golden brown. This should take about 10-15 minutes.
Once the coconut mixture has thickened and turned golden brown, reduce the heat to low. Add the vanilla extract and a pinch of salt, if desired, for added flavor. Stir the mixture continuously over low heat for another 2-3 minutes, until it forms a cohesive mass and starts to pull away from the sides of the skillet.
Remove the skillet from the heat and let the coconut candy mixture cool slightly for a few minutes.
While the mixture is still warm but manageable, use a spoon or your hands to shape the coconut candy into small balls or any desired shapes.
Place the shaped coconut candies on a parchment-lined baking sheet or plate to cool completely and set.
Once the coconut candies have cooled and set, they are ready to be enjoyed! Serve them as a sweet snack or dessert.

Store any leftover coconut candies in an airtight container at room temperature for up to a week. Enjoy the delicious and coconutty taste of Nigerian Coconut Candy!

Nigerian Moi Moi Roll

Ingredients:

- 2 cups peeled black-eyed peas
- 1 onion, chopped
- 2-3 tomatoes, chopped
- 2-3 scotch bonnet peppers (adjust to taste)
- 3 cloves of garlic
- 1 thumb-sized piece of ginger, grated
- 1/2 cup vegetable oil
- 1/4 cup water
- 2 tablespoons ground crayfish (optional)
- 2 teaspoons bouillon powder or cubes
- Salt to taste
- Plantain leaves or aluminum foil for wrapping

Instructions:

Rinse the black-eyed peas thoroughly and soak them in water for at least 4 hours or overnight.

Drain the soaked black-eyed peas and transfer them to a blender or food processor.

Add chopped onions, tomatoes, scotch bonnet peppers, garlic, and ginger to the blender with the soaked black-eyed peas. Blend until you get a smooth paste, adding water as needed to facilitate blending.

Transfer the blended mixture to a mixing bowl. Add vegetable oil, ground crayfish (if using), bouillon powder or cubes, and salt to taste. Mix well to combine.

Prepare your plantain leaves or aluminum foil by cutting them into rectangles large enough to wrap the Moi Moi mixture.

Place a portion of the Moi Moi mixture onto each plantain leaf or foil rectangle. Roll the Moi Moi mixture tightly into a cylindrical shape, making sure to seal the edges.

Repeat the process until all of the Moi Moi mixture is used up.

Place the rolled Moi Moi on a steamer rack or baking tray, seam side down.

Steam the Moi Moi rolls over medium heat for about 45-60 minutes, or until set and firm to the touch. Alternatively, you can bake them in a preheated oven at 350°F (175°C) for about 45-60 minutes.

Once cooked, remove the Moi Moi rolls from the steamer or oven and let them cool slightly before unwrapping.
Unwrap the Moi Moi rolls and slice them into rounds or serve them whole.
Serve the Nigerian Moi Moi rolls warm or at room temperature as a delicious and nutritious snack or side dish.

Enjoy the unique and flavorful twist of Nigerian Moi Moi Roll! Feel free to customize the recipe by adding other ingredients such as shredded vegetables or cooked meats according to your taste preferences.

Nigerian Banga Soup

Ingredients:

- 2 cups palm nut extract (banga juice) - you can use canned or freshly squeezed palm nut extract
- Assorted meats (such as beef, goat meat, or chicken), cut into bite-sized pieces
- Smoked fish or dried fish, flaked
- 1 onion, chopped
- 2-3 tomatoes, chopped
- 2-3 scotch bonnet peppers (adjust to taste), chopped
- 3 cloves of garlic, minced
- 1 thumb-sized piece of ginger, grated
- 1/4 cup crayfish, ground
- 1/4 cup periwinkle (optional)
- 2 tablespoons ground uziza seeds or ground dried bitterleaf (optional, for extra flavor)
- 1/4 cup palm oil
- Salt and pepper to taste
- Stock cubes or powder (optional)

Instructions:

In a large pot or Dutch oven, combine the palm nut extract (banga juice) with about 4 cups of water. Bring to a gentle boil over medium heat, then reduce the heat and let it simmer for about 30-45 minutes, stirring occasionally. This helps to cook the palm nut extract and reduce its bitterness.

While the palm nut extract is simmering, prepare the meats by seasoning them with salt, pepper, and any other desired spices. You can also boil the meats separately until they are partially cooked.

In a separate skillet or frying pan, heat palm oil over medium heat. Add chopped onions to the skillet and sauté until translucent.

Stir in minced garlic and grated ginger, and cook for another minute until fragrant. Add chopped tomatoes and scotch bonnet peppers to the skillet. Cook for about 10-15 minutes, stirring occasionally, until the tomatoes break down and release their juices.

Once the palm nut extract has simmered and reduced, add the cooked meats, smoked fish or dried fish, and the sautéed tomato mixture to the pot. Stir well to combine.

Add ground crayfish and periwinkle (if using) to the pot. Also, add ground uziza seeds or ground dried bitterleaf (if using) for extra flavor.

Season the Banga Soup with salt and pepper to taste. You can also add stock cubes or powder for additional flavor, if desired.

Let the Banga Soup simmer for another 20-30 minutes, stirring occasionally, to allow the flavors to meld together and the meats to become tender.

Once the Banga Soup is cooked to your liking, remove it from the heat.

Serve the Nigerian Banga Soup hot with a side of fufu, pounded yam, or rice.

Enjoy the rich and flavorful taste of Nigerian Banga Soup, filled with the goodness of palm nut extract, assorted meats, and spices! Feel free to customize the recipe by adding other ingredients such as vegetables or seafood according to your taste preferences.

Nigerian Vegetable Sauce

Ingredients:

- 2 cups chopped mixed vegetables (such as carrots, bell peppers, green beans, cabbage, and spinach)
- 1 onion, chopped
- 2-3 tomatoes, chopped
- 2-3 scotch bonnet peppers (adjust to taste), chopped
- 3 cloves of garlic, minced
- 1 thumb-sized piece of ginger, grated
- 1/4 cup palm oil or vegetable oil
- 1 teaspoon curry powder
- 1 teaspoon thyme
- 1 teaspoon paprika
- 2 cups vegetable broth or water
- Salt and pepper to taste
- Fresh cilantro or parsley for garnish (optional)

Instructions:

In a large skillet or frying pan, heat palm oil or vegetable oil over medium heat.
Add chopped onions to the skillet and sauté until translucent.
Stir in minced garlic and grated ginger, and cook for another minute until fragrant.
Add chopped tomatoes and scotch bonnet peppers to the skillet. Cook for about 10-15 minutes, stirring occasionally, until the tomatoes break down and release their juices.
Add chopped mixed vegetables to the skillet. Cook for about 5-10 minutes, stirring occasionally, until the vegetables are slightly softened.
Stir in curry powder, thyme, and paprika, and cook for another minute to toast the spices.
Pour in vegetable broth or water into the skillet, enough to cover the vegetables. Bring the mixture to a gentle simmer.
Let the Vegetable Sauce simmer for about 10-15 minutes, or until the vegetables are cooked to your desired tenderness and the sauce has thickened slightly.
Season the sauce with salt and pepper to taste.
Once the Vegetable Sauce is cooked to your liking, remove it from the heat.

Garnish the Nigerian Vegetable Sauce with fresh cilantro or parsley, if desired, before serving.

Serve the Nigerian Vegetable Sauce hot with rice, yams, plantains, or any other preferred side dish. Enjoy the flavorful and nutritious taste of this classic Nigerian dish! Feel free to customize the recipe by adding other vegetables or spices according to your taste preferences.

Nigerian Ofada Rice and Ayamase Stew

Ofada Rice:

Ingredients:

- 2 cups ofada rice
- Water for soaking and cooking
- Salt to taste

Instructions:

Rinse the ofada rice thoroughly in cold water to remove any dirt or debris.
Place the rinsed rice in a bowl and cover it with water. Allow it to soak for at least 30 minutes to 1 hour.
Drain the soaked rice and transfer it to a pot. Add enough water to cover the rice by about an inch.
Bring the water to a boil over high heat, then reduce the heat to low and let the rice simmer, covered, for about 30-40 minutes, or until the rice is tender but still firm.
Once the rice is cooked, drain any excess water and fluff the rice with a fork. Season with salt to taste, if desired.

Ayamase Stew

Ingredients:

- Assorted meats (such as beef, tripe, or cow foot), cut into bite-sized pieces
- 1 onion, chopped
- 2-3 tomatoes, chopped
- 2-3 bell peppers (red, yellow, or green), chopped
- 2-3 scotch bonnet peppers (adjust to taste), chopped
- 3 cloves of garlic, minced
- 1 thumb-sized piece of ginger, grated
- 1/4 cup palm oil or vegetable oil
- 2 tablespoons ground crayfish
- 1 teaspoon ground dried fish or smoked fish (optional)
- 2 cups beef broth or water
- Salt and pepper to taste
- Seasoning cubes or powder (optional)

Instructions:

In a large pot or Dutch oven, heat palm oil or vegetable oil over medium heat.
Add chopped onions to the pot and sauté until translucent.
Stir in minced garlic and grated ginger, and cook for another minute until fragrant.
Add chopped tomatoes, bell peppers, and scotch bonnet peppers to the pot.
Cook for about 10-15 minutes, stirring occasionally, until the vegetables are softened and release their juices.
Add the assorted meats to the pot and coat them with the tomato mixture. Cook for a few minutes until the meats are browned.
Stir in ground crayfish and ground dried fish or smoked fish (if using). Cook for another minute to enhance the flavors.
Pour in beef broth or water into the pot, enough to cover the ingredients. Bring the mixture to a gentle simmer.
Let the Ayamase Stew simmer for about 45-60 minutes, or until the meats are tender and the sauce has thickened.
Season the stew with salt, pepper, and seasoning cubes or powder to taste.
Once the Ayamase Stew is cooked to your liking, remove it from the heat.

Serve the Nigerian Ofada Rice and Ayamase Stew together as a delicious and satisfying meal. Enjoy the rich and spicy flavors of this classic Nigerian dish! Adjust the seasoning and spiciness according to your taste preferences.

Nigerian Afang Soup

Ingredients:

- 2 cups shredded afang leaves (substitute with spinach or other leafy greens if unavailable)
- 1 cup waterleaf (substitute with pumpkin leaves or spinach if unavailable)
- Assorted meats (such as beef, cow tripe, or assorted offals), cut into bite-sized pieces
- Smoked fish or dried fish, flaked
- 1 onion, chopped
- 2-3 tomatoes, chopped
- 2-3 scotch bonnet peppers (adjust to taste), chopped
- 3 cloves of garlic, minced
- 1 thumb-sized piece of ginger, grated
- 1/4 cup palm oil
- 1/4 cup ground crayfish
- 2 cups meat or seafood broth (or water)
- Salt and pepper to taste
- Stock cubes or powder (optional)

Instructions:

In a large pot or Dutch oven, heat palm oil over medium heat.
Add chopped onions to the pot and sauté until translucent.
Stir in minced garlic and grated ginger, and cook for another minute until fragrant.
Add chopped tomatoes and scotch bonnet peppers to the pot. Cook for about 10-15 minutes, stirring occasionally, until the tomatoes break down and release their juices.
Add the assorted meats to the pot and coat them with the tomato mixture. Cook for a few minutes until the meats are browned.
Stir in ground crayfish and flaked smoked fish or dried fish. Cook for another minute to enhance the flavors.
Pour in meat or seafood broth (or water) into the pot, enough to cover the ingredients. Bring the mixture to a gentle simmer.
Add the shredded afang leaves and waterleaf to the pot. Stir well to combine.
Let the Afang Soup simmer for about 20-30 minutes, or until the vegetables are cooked to your desired tenderness.
Season the soup with salt, pepper, and stock cubes or powder to taste.

Once the Afang Soup is cooked to your liking, remove it from the heat.

Serve the Nigerian Afang Soup hot with a side of fufu, pounded yam, or rice. Enjoy the rich and flavorful taste of this classic Nigerian dish! Feel free to customize the recipe by adding other ingredients such as periwinkle or snails according to your taste preferences.

Nigerian Gizzdodo (Gizzard and Plantain)

Ingredients:

- 500g chicken or turkey gizzards, cleaned and cut into bite-sized pieces
- 3 ripe plantains, peeled and cut into cubes
- 2 bell peppers (red, yellow, or green), diced
- 1 onion, chopped
- 3-4 tomatoes, chopped
- 2-3 scotch bonnet peppers (adjust to taste), chopped
- 3 cloves of garlic, minced
- 1 thumb-sized piece of ginger, grated
- 1/4 cup vegetable oil
- 1 teaspoon curry powder
- 1 teaspoon thyme
- 1 teaspoon paprika
- Salt and pepper to taste
- Fresh cilantro or parsley for garnish (optional)

Instructions:

In a large skillet or frying pan, heat vegetable oil over medium heat.
Add the chopped onions to the skillet and sauté until translucent.
Stir in minced garlic and grated ginger, and cook for another minute until fragrant.
Add the diced bell peppers and chopped tomatoes to the skillet. Cook for about 10-15 minutes, stirring occasionally, until the vegetables are softened and release their juices.
Add the chopped scotch bonnet peppers to the skillet, along with curry powder, thyme, and paprika. Stir well to combine.
Add the cleaned and chopped gizzards to the skillet. Cook for about 15-20 minutes, stirring occasionally, until the gizzards are cooked through and tender.
While the gizzards are cooking, heat vegetable oil in a separate frying pan over medium heat. Fry the cubed plantains until golden brown and caramelized. Remove from the oil and drain on paper towels.
Once the gizzards are cooked, add the fried plantains to the skillet with the gizzards and vegetables. Stir well to combine.
Season the Gizzdodo with salt and pepper to taste. Adjust the seasoning as needed.

Let the Gizzdodo simmer for another 5-10 minutes, stirring occasionally, to allow the flavors to meld together.

Once the Gizzdodo is cooked to your liking, remove it from the heat.

Garnish the Nigerian Gizzdodo with fresh cilantro or parsley, if desired, before serving.

Serve the Gizzdodo hot as a delicious and satisfying meal or appetizer. Enjoy the rich and flavorful taste of this classic Nigerian dish! Feel free to customize the recipe by adding other ingredients such as carrots or green peas according to your taste preferences.

Nigerian Yam Porridge

Ingredients:

- 1 medium-sized yam, peeled and cut into cubes
- 1 onion, chopped
- 2-3 tomatoes, chopped
- 2-3 scotch bonnet peppers (adjust to taste), chopped
- 3 cloves of garlic, minced
- 1 thumb-sized piece of ginger, grated
- 1/4 cup palm oil or vegetable oil
- Assorted meats or fish (such as beef, chicken, or smoked fish), cut into bite-sized pieces (optional)
- 2 cups vegetable broth or water
- 1 teaspoon ground crayfish (optional)
- 1 teaspoon ground dried fish or smoked fish (optional)
- Salt and pepper to taste
- Stock cubes or powder (optional)
- Fresh cilantro or parsley for garnish (optional)

Instructions:

In a large pot or Dutch oven, heat palm oil or vegetable oil over medium heat.
Add chopped onions to the pot and sauté until translucent.
Stir in minced garlic and grated ginger, and cook for another minute until fragrant.
Add chopped tomatoes and scotch bonnet peppers to the pot. Cook for about 10-15 minutes, stirring occasionally, until the tomatoes break down and release their juices.
If using assorted meats or fish, add them to the pot and cook until browned.
Add the cubed yam to the pot. Stir well to coat the yam with the tomato mixture.
Pour in vegetable broth or water into the pot, enough to cover the yam. Bring the mixture to a gentle simmer.
Let the Yam Porridge simmer for about 20-25 minutes, or until the yam is tender and cooked through.
Stir in ground crayfish and ground dried fish or smoked fish (if using). Season the porridge with salt, pepper, and stock cubes or powder to taste.
Once the Yam Porridge is cooked to your liking and the sauce has thickened, remove it from the heat.

Serve the Nigerian Yam Porridge hot, garnished with fresh cilantro or parsley if desired.

Enjoy the comforting and flavorful taste of Nigerian Yam Porridge! Feel free to customize the recipe by adding other vegetables such as spinach or kale, or by adjusting the spices according to your taste preferences.

Nigerian Asun (Spicy Goat Meat)

Ingredients:

- 1 kg (about 2.2 lbs) goat meat, cut into bite-sized pieces
- 2 onions, finely chopped
- 3-4 scotch bonnet peppers (adjust to taste), finely chopped
- 3 cloves of garlic, minced
- 1 thumb-sized piece of ginger, grated
- 2 tablespoons ground crayfish (optional)
- 2 tablespoons ground dried fish or smoked fish (optional)
- 1/4 cup palm oil or vegetable oil
- Salt to taste
- Stock cubes or powder (optional)
- Fresh cilantro or parsley for garnish (optional)
- Lime or lemon wedges for serving (optional)

Instructions:

In a large bowl, season the goat meat with chopped onions, scotch bonnet peppers, minced garlic, grated ginger, ground crayfish, ground dried fish or smoked fish (if using), and salt to taste. Mix well to ensure that the meat is evenly coated with the seasonings. You can also add stock cubes or powder for additional flavor, if desired. Marinate the meat for at least 1-2 hours, or overnight in the refrigerator, to allow the flavors to develop.

Preheat your grill or barbecue to medium-high heat. Alternatively, you can use an oven broiler or a stovetop grill pan.

Thread the seasoned goat meat onto skewers, leaving a little space between each piece to ensure even cooking.

Grill the skewered goat meat for about 10-15 minutes on each side, or until cooked through and slightly charred. Alternatively, if using an oven broiler, place the skewers on a baking sheet and broil for about 10-15 minutes on each side until cooked and slightly charred.

While the goat meat is grilling, heat palm oil or vegetable oil in a large skillet or frying pan over medium heat.

Once the goat meat is cooked, remove it from the skewers and transfer it to the skillet with the heated oil. Fry the goat meat in the oil for about 5-7 minutes, stirring occasionally, until it is well coated with the oil and slightly crispy on the edges.

Remove the skillet from the heat and transfer the fried goat meat to a serving platter.

Garnish the Nigerian Asun with fresh cilantro or parsley, if desired. Serve hot with lime or lemon wedges on the side for squeezing over the meat for added flavor.

Enjoy the spicy and flavorful taste of Nigerian Asun as a delicious appetizer or side dish at your next gathering or special occasion! Adjust the level of spiciness according to your taste preferences by increasing or decreasing the amount of scotch bonnet peppers used.

Nigerian Fisherman Soup

Ingredients:

- Assorted seafood (such as whole fish, prawns, crab, and/or mussels), cleaned and deveined
- 2 onions, chopped
- 2-3 tomatoes, chopped
- 2-3 scotch bonnet peppers (adjust to taste), chopped
- 3 cloves of garlic, minced
- 1 thumb-sized piece of ginger, grated
- 1/4 cup palm oil or vegetable oil
- 2 cups fish or seafood broth (or water)
- 2 tablespoons ground crayfish
- 1 teaspoon ground dried fish or smoked fish (optional)
- 2 cups chopped leafy greens (such as spinach or kale)
- Salt and pepper to taste
- Stock cubes or powder (optional)
- Fresh cilantro or parsley for garnish (optional)

Instructions:

In a large pot or Dutch oven, heat palm oil or vegetable oil over medium heat.
Add chopped onions to the pot and sauté until translucent.
Stir in minced garlic and grated ginger, and cook for another minute until fragrant.
Add chopped tomatoes and scotch bonnet peppers to the pot. Cook for about 10-15 minutes, stirring occasionally, until the tomatoes break down and release their juices.
If using ground dried fish or smoked fish, add it to the pot along with ground crayfish. Stir well to combine.
Pour in fish or seafood broth (or water) into the pot, enough to cover the ingredients. Bring the mixture to a gentle simmer.
Add the assorted seafood to the pot. Cook for about 5-7 minutes, or until the seafood is cooked through and tender.
Stir in chopped leafy greens to the pot and let them cook for another 2-3 minutes, until wilted.
Season the Fisherman Soup with salt, pepper, and stock cubes or powder to taste.

Once the Fisherman Soup is cooked to your liking, remove it from the heat. Garnish the Nigerian Fisherman Soup with fresh cilantro or parsley, if desired, before serving.

Serve the Fisherman Soup hot with fufu, pounded yam, or rice. Enjoy the rich and aromatic taste of this classic Nigerian seafood soup! Feel free to customize the recipe by adding other seafood or vegetables according to your taste preferences.

Nigerian Beans Porridge (Beans Pottage)

Ingredients:

- 2 cups black-eyed peas or brown beans, rinsed and soaked overnight
- 1 onion, chopped
- 2-3 tomatoes, chopped
- 2-3 scotch bonnet peppers (adjust to taste), chopped
- 3 cloves of garlic, minced
- 1 thumb-sized piece of ginger, grated
- 1/4 cup palm oil or vegetable oil
- Assorted meats or fish (such as beef, smoked fish, or dried fish), cut into bite-sized pieces (optional)
- 2 cups vegetable broth or water
- 1 teaspoon ground crayfish (optional)
- 1 teaspoon ground dried fish or smoked fish (optional)
- Salt and pepper to taste
- Stock cubes or powder (optional)
- Fresh cilantro or parsley for garnish (optional)

Instructions:

Drain and rinse the soaked beans thoroughly. Place them in a large pot and cover with water. Bring to a boil over medium-high heat, then reduce the heat and let them simmer for about 45 minutes to 1 hour, or until tender. Alternatively, you can cook the beans in a pressure cooker for faster results.

While the beans are cooking, heat palm oil or vegetable oil in a large skillet or frying pan over medium heat.

Add chopped onions to the skillet and sauté until translucent.

Stir in minced garlic and grated ginger, and cook for another minute until fragrant.

Add chopped tomatoes and scotch bonnet peppers to the skillet. Cook for about 10-15 minutes, stirring occasionally, until the tomatoes break down and release their juices.

If using assorted meats or fish, add them to the skillet and cook until browned.

Once the beans are tender, drain any excess water and add them to the skillet with the cooked tomatoes and peppers. Stir well to combine.

Pour in vegetable broth or water into the skillet, enough to cover the beans. Bring the mixture to a gentle simmer.

Add ground crayfish and ground dried fish or smoked fish (if using). Season the beans with salt, pepper, and stock cubes or powder to taste.

Let the Beans Porridge simmer for about 10-15 minutes, stirring occasionally, to allow the flavors to meld together and the beans to absorb the seasonings.

Once the Beans Porridge reaches your desired consistency, remove it from the heat.

Garnish the Nigerian Beans Porridge with fresh cilantro or parsley, if desired, before serving.

Serve the Beans Porridge hot as a delicious and nutritious meal or side dish. Enjoy the rich and satisfying taste of this classic Nigerian dish! Feel free to customize the recipe by adding other ingredients such as spinach or pumpkin leaves according to your taste preferences.

Nigerian Fish Roll

Ingredients:

For the pastry dough:

- 2 cups all-purpose flour
- 1/4 cup granulated sugar
- 1/2 teaspoon salt
- 1 teaspoon baking powder
- 1/2 cup unsalted butter, cold and cut into small cubes
- 1/4 cup cold water
- 1 egg, beaten (for egg wash)

For the fish filling:

- 1 cup cooked and flaked fish (such as mackerel or tilapia)
- 1 onion, finely chopped
- 2 cloves of garlic, minced
- 1 teaspoon ground paprika
- 1 teaspoon ground cumin
- Salt and pepper to taste
- Vegetable oil for frying

Instructions:

In a large mixing bowl, combine the all-purpose flour, granulated sugar, salt, and baking powder. Mix well.

Add the cold, cubed unsalted butter to the flour mixture. Use your fingertips to rub the butter into the flour until the mixture resembles coarse breadcrumbs.

Gradually add the cold water to the flour mixture, a little at a time, and mix until a dough forms. Be careful not to overwork the dough.

Transfer the dough onto a lightly floured surface and knead gently for a few minutes until smooth. Wrap the dough in plastic wrap and refrigerate for about 30 minutes to firm up.

While the dough is chilling, prepare the fish filling. In a skillet, heat a little vegetable oil over medium heat. Add the chopped onion and minced garlic and sauté until softened.

Add the cooked and flaked fish to the skillet, along with ground paprika, ground cumin, salt, and pepper to taste. Stir well to combine and cook for another 2-3 minutes. Remove from heat and let the filling cool.

Preheat your oven to 350°F (175°C). Line a baking sheet with parchment paper. Remove the chilled dough from the refrigerator and roll it out on a lightly floured surface to about 1/4 inch thickness.

Use a round cookie cutter or the rim of a glass to cut out circles from the dough. Place a spoonful of the cooled fish filling in the center of each dough circle.

Fold the dough over the filling to create a half-moon shape and seal the edges by pressing them together with a fork.

Place the filled fish rolls on the prepared baking sheet. Brush the tops of the rolls with beaten egg wash.

Bake in the preheated oven for about 20-25 minutes, or until the rolls are golden brown and crispy.

Once baked, remove the fish rolls from the oven and let them cool slightly before serving.

Serve the Nigerian Fish Rolls warm as a delicious snack or appetizer.

Enjoy the crispy pastry and flavorful fish filling of these homemade Nigerian Fish Rolls!

Adjust the seasoning and spices in the filling according to your taste preferences.

Nigerian Prawn Stir Fry

Ingredients:

- 500g large prawns (shrimp), peeled and deveined
- 1 onion, thinly sliced
- 1 bell pepper (red, green, or yellow), thinly sliced
- 1 carrot, julienned
- 1 cup snap peas or green beans, trimmed
- 3 cloves of garlic, minced
- 1 thumb-sized piece of ginger, grated
- 2 tablespoons soy sauce
- 1 tablespoon oyster sauce
- 1 tablespoon honey or brown sugar
- 2 tablespoons vegetable oil
- Salt and pepper to taste
- Fresh cilantro or parsley for garnish (optional)
- Cooked rice or noodles for serving

Instructions:

In a small bowl, mix together the soy sauce, oyster sauce, and honey (or brown sugar). Set aside.
Heat vegetable oil in a large skillet or wok over medium-high heat.
Add the sliced onion to the skillet and stir-fry for 1-2 minutes until softened.
Add the minced garlic and grated ginger to the skillet. Stir-fry for another minute until fragrant.
Add the sliced bell pepper, julienned carrot, and snap peas (or green beans) to the skillet. Stir-fry for 3-4 minutes until the vegetables are slightly softened but still crisp.
Push the vegetables to one side of the skillet and add the prawns to the empty side. Cook the prawns for 2-3 minutes on each side until pink and cooked through.
Pour the prepared sauce over the prawns and vegetables in the skillet. Stir well to coat everything evenly with the sauce.
Continue to cook for another 1-2 minutes until the sauce thickens slightly and coats the prawns and vegetables.
Season the Prawn Stir Fry with salt and pepper to taste.

Once cooked, remove the skillet from the heat.
Serve the Nigerian Prawn Stir Fry hot over cooked rice or noodles.
Garnish with fresh cilantro or parsley, if desired, before serving.

Enjoy the delicious and flavorful Nigerian Prawn Stir Fry as a quick and satisfying meal!

Feel free to customize the recipe by adding other vegetables or adjusting the seasonings according to your taste preferences.

Nigerian Chicken Shawarma

Ingredients:

For the Chicken Marinade:

- 500g boneless chicken breasts or thighs, thinly sliced
- 1/4 cup plain yogurt
- 2 tablespoons olive oil
- 3 cloves garlic, minced
- 1 teaspoon ground cumin
- 1 teaspoon paprika
- 1/2 teaspoon ground turmeric
- Salt and pepper to taste

For the Shawarma Sauce:

- 1/2 cup mayonnaise
- 2 tablespoons plain yogurt
- 1 tablespoon lemon juice
- 1 teaspoon ground cumin
- 1 teaspoon paprika
- Salt and pepper to taste

For Assembly:

- Flatbreads or pita bread
- Sliced tomatoes
- Sliced cucumbers
- Shredded lettuce or cabbage
- Sliced onions
- Pickles (optional)
- Hot sauce or chili sauce (optional)

Instructions:

In a bowl, combine the ingredients for the chicken marinade: plain yogurt, olive oil, minced garlic, ground cumin, paprika, turmeric, salt, and pepper. Mix well. Add the thinly sliced chicken to the marinade and toss until evenly coated. Cover and refrigerate for at least 30 minutes, or longer if possible.

While the chicken is marinating, prepare the shawarma sauce. In a small bowl, mix together mayonnaise, plain yogurt, lemon juice, ground cumin, paprika, salt, and pepper. Adjust seasoning to taste. Set aside.

Heat a grill pan or skillet over medium-high heat. Add a drizzle of oil.

Remove the marinated chicken from the refrigerator and grill in the pan for about 4-5 minutes on each side, or until cooked through and charred. You can also use an outdoor grill or broiler.

Once cooked, remove the chicken from the heat and let it rest for a few minutes.

Warm the flatbreads or pita bread in the oven or on a skillet.

To assemble the shawarma, spread a generous amount of shawarma sauce onto each flatbread or pita bread.

Place a portion of grilled chicken on top of the sauce, followed by sliced tomatoes, cucumbers, onions, shredded lettuce or cabbage, and pickles if using.

Drizzle with additional shawarma sauce and hot sauce or chili sauce if desired.

Roll up the flatbread or pita bread tightly, enclosing the filling.

Serve the Nigerian Chicken Shawarma immediately, either whole or sliced into smaller portions.

Enjoy your delicious homemade Nigerian Chicken Shawarma! Feel free to customize the fillings and adjust the seasoning according to your taste preferences.